# Joy & Pain:
## Living with Sickle Cell Anemia

Samantha R. Williams

© 2020 Samantha R. Williams
Joy & Pain: Living with Sickle Cell Anemia
Kingdom Builders Publications, LLC

All rights reserved. No part of this book may be reproduced or transmitted in any form or by any means without written permission from the author.

\* All Scriptures are taken from the King James Version.

Printed in the USA

ISBN 978-057-868505-2 Soft Cover

**Authored by**
Samantha R. Williams

**Editor**
Dr. Lakisha S. Forrester
Kingdom Builders Publications

**Cover Design**
LoMar Designs

**Picture for cover**
ID 13727377 © Jennifer Pitiquen | Dreamstime.com

# DEDICATION

I dedicate this book to my two sisters with whom I shared this illness, Darlene and Antoinette. Although you both have transitioned home to be with our Lord, there is not one day that goes by that I don't think of you two. Your life on this earth was relatively short. But, I will always treasure the times I got to be around you. We shared our bedroom – doing hair, talking about school and boys, and comparing our hospital treatments. Oh those precious memories are near and dear to my heart, and they keep me going. Both of you gave me a lot to look up to. I am very proud to have had you as my big sisters.

# FOREWORD

I remember that day in 2019 when Samantha had a sickle cell crisis. I walked nervously throughout the hospital's halls unaware of what I might find when I enter her room. But, just like that tenacious Samantha that existed before this hospital visit, she was alright. She was in such good spirits and had the biggest grin on her face even with tubes and IV lines connected to her veins. I was even more astonished when the nurse came into the room to check on her progress. Samantha spouted out her own vital signs to the nurse and told her how many cc's of which medicine she was going to need. I was simply impressed by her thoroughness but even more in awe of her journey.

Samantha is truly a soldier at heart. She possesses such beauty and strength that you know comes from the Lord Almighty Savior. Even before that day, I never saw her not smile or not give God the glory regardless of circumstances or how much pain she was in. She is definitely no complainer but a celebrator of life.

I am simply proud, impressed, and thankful to Samantha for writing this book and being able to share her story with the world.

*Dr. Lakisha S. Forrester*
*Sister in Christ*

# CONTENTS

| | |
|---|---|
| Dedication | iii |
| Foreword | iv |
| Preface | vii |
| Opening Prayer | viii |
| Acknowledgments | ix |
| Introduction | xi |
| The Story of My Life | 12 |
| The Crisis | 13 |
| The Early Years | 14 |
| My Working Days | 15 |
| Our Secret | 17 |
| A Devastating Passing | 18 |
| A Renewed Strength | 18 |
| Not Again | 19 |
| Defying the Odds | 19 |
| A New Season | 20 |
| The Confession | 20 |
| Being Fruitful | 21 |
| The Talk – Q & A | 25 |

| | |
|---|---|
| What Now? | 28 |
| God's Unchanging Hand | 28 |
| More Complications | 30 |
| Navigating Through the Journey | 34 |
| God's Solution | 35 |
| Letters to My Children | 37 |
| Closing Prayer | 40 |
| About the Author | 41 |
| Resources | 43 |

# PREFACE

I always dreamed of writing a book. I just didn't know the day or the hour. Since my life revolved around sickle cell anemia, I said to myself, *Why not write about it?* So I began to release my thoughts and these words that have been bottled up inside of me for years. I want to thank God for putting the desire to write this book in my spirit at this appointed time.

# OPENING PRAYER

*Dear Heavenly Father,*

*Thank you for life, health, and strength. Thank you for allowing me to stand in the gap and intercede on behalf of parents who have children with sickle cell anemia.*

*Lord, I ask you to please give them strength when their children are in "crisis" and cannot attend school or have to be hospitalized.*

*God, I ask that you would continue to provide joy and peace in the hearts of your precious ones diagnosed and enduring this disease. Keep a song in their hearts and a smile on their faces.*

*God, please give favor in the classrooms with the teachers. Let them be filled with compassion towards these children.*

*Lord, as they grow and develop, put people in their lives that will build them up and understand when they are just not feeling too great. Provide them with someone they can trust and feel free to share some personal health information so they would have help in case of an emergency.*

*In Jesus' name I pray,*

*Amen.*

# ACKNOWLEDGMENTS

Thank you, Mr. James Jackson (Daddy), I am who I am because of you. You believed in me and affirmed me every day while you were on this earth. You have taught me, but most of all, Daddy, you LOVED me. Daddy, whenever I would leave the house, you would tell me to go down there, mind my own business, keep my mouth closed, and come back home. Those were the best instructions a girl could ever have gotten. Thanks, Daddy. I love and miss you so much.

A special thank you to my mom, brothers, and sisters – FAMILY is forever. Remember, no matter who, what, when, and how, WE are stronger together. Much Love.

To my heartbeats, Jocelynn D'Antoinette, Titus Alexander, and Benjamin Luke, writing this book about the story of my life was a surreal process for me. Please know you bring me joy. Continue to love each other and don't forget that a three-strand cord is NOT easily broken (Ecclesiastes 4:12). Now I can add author to my résumé; but, there are no accomplishments or accolades better than being your Mother. I love you always.

Ted, you took the ride with me, hospital after hospital and doctor after doctor. With every visit, you lived out our wedding vows, "In Sickness and In Health." It gave me peace to know that you were there, no matter if it was 1 a.m., 3 a.m., 5 a.m., etc. Now that's LOVE.

Rho (Mother), I love and miss you. From the lessons you taught me, the shopping trips, and the food we ate together, my life was better because of you. I thank God for allowing us to meet. I know it was not by chance but a divine appointment. I will forever cherish every memory that I hold dear to my heart. Hands down, you were the best Godmother a girl like me could ever have.

To my squad, Syreeta, Giselle, Sharen, Joyce, Barbara, Tracey, Aunt Angye, Mom Porter, Kisha, Tina, and Timica, you have seen me at my best and worst and never once judged me, laughed at me, talked about me, or not offer to help me. And for that I say, Thank You. Your love is felt daily. Even though some of us are miles and states apart, distance never changed a thing. All of you demonstrate the love and faithfulness found in Matthew 25:35-40 and John 13:35.

# INTRODUCTION

Living with sickle cell anemia has brought many challenges in my life. Challenges that sometimes I felt were so unfair. Challenges that made me mad some days and happy other days. I don't understand it all and I sure do not know it all. But, I do know that I am loved by my husband, my children, my family, and my friends. But above all else, I'm loved by God…so what else could I really ask for?

The older I get, I like to celebrate every year of my birth because I was always told that I would not make it to see forty. Yet here I am, in my fifties, thanking God for extending my life beyond man's statistics. To God Be the Glory! I feel like my life is being used as a testimony to show people who God is. I remember the story of Jesus healing a man who was born blind. Because the man was born blind, the disciples implied that either the man sinned or his parents sinned. Inquisitively, they asked Jesus who was the sin culprit. Jesus replied that sin was not the cause of this issue, but this happened so that it would be obvious that this was the handiwork of God (John 9:1-12).

# THE STORY OF MY LIFE

I was born and raised in West Philadelphia, PA. At a relatively young age, I will never forget the day when my life changed and nothing was ever the same again.

I remember like it was yesterday when the doctor told my mom that I have sickle cell disease and that I will have to take medicine for the rest of my life. *How can that be possible? I am only 11 years old.* My mom had so many questions, but she was given little to no answers. The one question I wanted somebody or anybody to answer was... *Why?*

I spent a great deal of my life in the hospital, at least two to three times a year for sickle cell anemia. This disease has caused my red blood cells to sickle, or form a shape that's reminiscent of a crescent moon. So as a result, my blood and oxygen are blocked from flowing properly to my cells. As you can imagine, this causes me to have an intense amount of pain throughout my body. In addition to this disease, I also have pulmonary hypertension and atrial fibrillation (AFib), which means that the atrial chambers of my heart beat so fast and irregularly that not all of my blood gets pumped from the atria into the ventricles.

## THE CRISIS

I will never forget the day when my blood count dropped so low that I needed to have a blood transfusion. I stayed in the emergency room for three days and two nights before being transferred to the intermediate intensive care unit. Once I got to my designated room, things began to happen very quickly. The pain from my "sickle cell crisis," as we call it, began to ease up.

As I looked at the blood hanging on a pole with a direct line into my vein, all I could think about was that song we sang in church that talked about the precious blood of the Lamb. At the time, I really didn't think that all that blood was going to be used to replenish my body. The only thing I thought about was Jesus hanging from a cross with His blood pouring out for us all. At that moment, tears began to flow down my face. I just thought about how He bled and died for my sins (even sins I had yet to commit) and rose again because He thought I was worth it. And if you don't know it, my dearly beloved reader, you are worth it as well. I am standing here today only because of God's grace. I don't know why He chose for me to be here this long with illnesses that can lead to an early death, but in the midst of the pain from my poorly constricted and flowing blood, I am still grateful. Why? Because I know that His blood flows through my veins as well. His blood is the sustaining blood, the everlasting blood, the powerful blood, the almighty blood. Oh yes, His blood gets me through day to day.

## THE EARLY YEARS

I struggled in my early years with this disease. Fatigue and nausea were a constant. I felt like I was always chucking my guts out. Of course, school was very challenging because I never knew if I was going to make it through the entire day without getting sick.

In the beginning, I hated living with sickle cell anemia. Every time I went to the doctor, I was always told what I could or should not be able to do. The one thing that disturbed me the most was when the doctor uttered these words, "Samantha, you can't have children." For years, I struggled with that statement because sickle cell was known as the "black people's disease." There wasn't much research going on at that time so I wondered how he could be so sure enough to tell me with certainty that I wouldn't be able to have children.

Through many years of emergency hospital visits, I've learned to listen and pay close attention to my body so that I could express what I felt on the inside to the doctors and nurses. Back then, it always felt like I had something that even the smart people, a.k.a. the doctors, did not know much about or even what to do with this disease and me.

I looked fine on the outside, but struggling with pain on the inside. As I began puberty, things really started happening. Sickle cell kicked into high gear. Sometimes the pain from my menstrual cycle was so bad that I would go into a crisis and have to be hospitalized.

## MY WORKING DAYS

When I was sixteen years old, I began working and was having the time of my life. I was earning money, meeting new people, and learning new things. But there were challenges when my "sidekick" showed up issuing bouts of fatigue to severe stomach pains. Those were generally the onset symptoms letting me know that I was going into crisis mode and that severe pain in my body would ensue in intensity. During those times, I would just think to myself as I worked on my shift, *Oh no, not now!* But, my body would say, *Oh yes, now!*

In any job I worked, whether it was in high school or as an adult, as a rule of thumb, I would always find one person to share my health issues with. I did that just in case I were to get sick and needed help. That designated person would know what to do for me, how to get me the correct help, and also get in touch with my family.

There was one job where I had to get a doctor's note stating that I had to be allowed to get up from my desk frequently and keep myself hydrated. At that time, I wasn't allowed to have anything on my desk to drink. With all the breaks I had to take to go to the water fountain, I'm simply amazed that the Lord allowed me to work at that job for over ten years. That's why I don't like water fountains to this day.

I feel that any type of sickness in my body, even the common cold, in my opinion, was ten times worse because of sickle cell anemia. I will never forget missing one of the most pivotal weeks in high school; it was the week of graduation practices. That week is one that every wide-eyed senior typically looks forward to with great anticipation of what's to come with the actual graduation, as well as his or her future after high school. Such an exciting time, right? Well, usually, but not exactly for me. At roll call, a teacher in charge of the practices stated, "Whoever knows Samantha, tell her if she misses any more graduation practices, she will not walk with the class on graduation day!" Well, of course that word got back to me and it saddened me greatly.

I thank God for my parents. My dad had to work, so my mom went to the school and explained that I was sick and that was why I was out of school that entire week. Needless to say, I graduated and walked across that stage. I was very happy to accomplish that goal and even more grateful to my parents for fighting for me.

## OUR SECRET

I remember when I found out that two of my sisters also had sickle cell anemia. I was baffled because I thought I was the only one with this disease. After the shock wore off, I began to experience a sense of pride. My sisters and I had this secret between us – "this disease" – that not everyone knew we had until we got sick. I just think about all the times of joy and pain that we shared together.

I will never forget the time when my sister Darlene got sick. At the hospital, the doctors were trying to figure out what was wrong with her. All of her tests were normal, so they decided to check for meningitis. In my sisterly protective mode and because I knew our "secret," I stepped up and said, "No, she is having a sickle cell crisis." When I look back on those times, I do believe that having this disease gave me a sense of boldness. I learned that it's not good to keep things bottled up inside, because anything or any stressors can cause you to go into crisis mode.

After the doctors ran more tests, they agreed that she, in fact, was having complications from sickle cell and they began to treat her with the proper medicine. As she began to come around and the symptoms of her crisis minimized, I felt really glad that I was able to help her.

## A DEVASTATING PASSING

At the age of 21, I found myself perplexed, shocked, and extremely sad as my family and I sat in the funeral home making preparations for my sister Antoinette's homegoing service. She was a sister, an aunt, a wife, and a mother. Initially, I couldn't figure out why she passed. So many emotions went through my body in the form of sadness, confusion, and anger. I felt like I was having an out of body experience. My mind never fathomed that this sickness could lead to death. I didn't know that this could possibly be the end result of what it could be like living with sickle cell.

I can honestly say that the business side of planning a funeral can be exhausting in and of itself (at least for me it was). I do remember that the staff was very nice. But, all I kept saying to myself was that I was in a funeral home because my sister died. It was just unbelievable to me. Accepting that my sister was no longer going to be here was a tough pill to swallow, and letting go was even harder for me.

## RENEWED STRENGTH

Heartbroken, confused, and wanting to give up were the staple thoughts in my head. I didn't think I had the will to go on after that. But, strength rose up in me as I faced what I considered to be the worst thing that could happen. So, I decided to keep working. I had to get my mind off it – well, at least I tried to. This made me realize that I had to live a more cautious lifestyle because I was only a scared twenty-four-year-old who just helped my family bury my sister. Yes, I was angry that this disease not only abruptly disrupted my life for thirteen years, but it took my beloved sister's life.

## NOT AGAIN

As the years passed, my sister Darlene and I began to bond more and look out for each other even more. We shared our hospital experiences every time either one of us was in there. We kept no secrets from each other; we discussed it all, from medicine to meals and everything in between. When sickle cell took her life at age fifty-seven, I felt all alone. Who was now going to be my confidant? Who was I going to share the joys and pains of my life with now? Those were the questions that I wrestled with. But, I didn't have any legitimate answers, other than to fight back. Antoinette and Darlene taught me how to be a trooper. I didn't want to let them down by bowing out early. So, I strategically decided that I would defy the odds, with the help of God, no matter what anyone said.

## DEFYING THE ODDS

Oh yes, I did it! I became a mother. Yes, it was a scary time because sickle cell was right there rearing its ugly head as usual, causing me to be hospitalized for an entire month before I gave birth to my one and only daughter, Jocelynn (whose name means joyful). That was the perfect name for her. Although I was in pain, I was full of joy knowing that I was told my life wouldn't result in having children and the exact opposite happened.

## A NEW SEASON

A few years later, I felt like it was a new season for me. I could only believe that the best was yet to come. I had a new love in my life and things were going well, or so I thought, until I got a call that my father had been rushed to the hospital. I will never forget that day for two reasons: That was the day my fiancé met my father; and unfortunately, that was also the same day my father died.

The next day, I went into a sickle cell crisis. I was in a coma for two weeks. By the time I woke up, my dad's homegoing had already taken place. I missed it; I didn't get to help bury my father. I believe God knew I wasn't going to be able to handle it.

## THE CONFESSION

I managed to keep the secret that I have sickle cell anemia from my fiancé for quite a while. I planned on telling him, but I got sick before that could happen.

While we were in the hospital room, my pastor encouraged me to share my medical history with my fiancé because it would not be fair for him to marry me not knowing that I had this somewhat debilitating disease.

I was very nervous and scared at the time, so I asked him to stay in the hospital room with me while I tell my fiancé all about it. He agreed to stay. Still in pain, with only an ounce of courage, I muttered these words to my fiancé after telling him about this disease, "If you marry me, we will be spending a lot of time in the hospital. If you don't want to marry me, I understand." I began to take off my engagement ring. He stopped me and told me he still wanted to marry me. I was so happy to hear that.

## BEING FRUITFUL

I already knew that I was at high risk being pregnant with my daughter, so I wasn't really trying to do that again. However, one day my husband and I talked about my health situation and he told me he wanted two kids.

This man done fell and bumped his head, is what I thought to myself. It's not like he wasn't aware of me being high risk. So, we agreed on having one child, and I was thankful about that.

Naturally, when my husband and I learned that we were expecting, we were overjoyed. Despite that, my happiness soon became entangled with fear, because I knew it wasn't going to be easy. But rather than constantly thinking about all the things that could possibly go wrong and getting ourselves upset, we chose to pray, believe, and put our trust in God.

Not long into my pregnancy, the doctor told us that our baby was in a crushed, amniotic sac and that my body would naturally abort the baby. The doctor also said there was no need to prescribe prenatal vitamins to me so she refused to give me any. We were absolutely devastated by that news. A close friend suggested that we get a second opinion, so we did. Our new doctor assured us that our baby was fine and not in a crushed sac. What a relief! I got my prenatal vitamins and life was good. I don't think I was ever that excited to take pills in my life.

Four months into my pregnancy, I started having contractions and had to be put on complete bed rest. I could not even walk to the bathroom by myself. The doctor ordered me an oxygen tank and a portable commode. I laid in that bed for three months before being hospitalized again.

Immediately after my child was born, because of complications from sickle cell, I had to have an emergency surgery to get the placenta removed. I received nine pints of blood that day. This was an extra special birth, in and of itself. The city of Philadelphia was offering money to parents for the first baby born in Y2K (Year 2000). I think the city decided to do that to bring a little hope to the people. There was so much havoc going on in the world then because of the fear that the technology would crash and cause governmental shutdowns. Regardless of the world's turmoil, my precious son, Titus Alexander, was born 12 hours earlier on New Year's Eve, weighing 2 pounds, 13 ounces, thus, disqualifying us from getting the money. However, we got something even more special in him; he was absolutely priceless.

I was so thankful to Jesus that I gave my husband a son. This began our first family tradition. My husband didn't want our son named after him, but he wanted him to have his same initials (T.A.W.) and same middle name. I truly felt like a winner and that we were on top of the world. Things calmed down for a while. We settled into our new lives as a family, with school and daycare on our priority list. I went back to work, and things were moving right along. My life felt like it was finally normal.

A few years later, when my stomach began hurting and I was vomiting, my first thought was, *Hello, sickle cell.* My husband took me to the hospital. Once again, the doctors ran several tests and asked me a whole lot of questions. The doctor looked at my husband and said, "Congratulations!" Instantly, my husband looked at me, and I looked at him. With a puzzled look on our faces, we both looked at the doctor. Then, the doctor said, "You're having a baby."

I didn't know what to do when I heard those words. I just got my body back to normal from having a baby two years prior. All I could do was pray because I was so scared that this time I might not be as fortunate and make it through the pregnancy.

I asked God to please get me through this without having so many sickle cell crises like I had with my other children. God heard my cry. My third pregnancy went fairly well up until my seventh month. After being in the hospital for three days, my son, Benjamin, was born on July 4th, weighing 4 pounds, 9 ounces.

That's it! No more for me, God! I was so thankful that I was able to give my husband the two children that he asked for, and I didn't die in the process. But God! As my children began to attend school, I missed out on some after school events and parent-teacher conferences because I was either sick or hospitalized. To this day, that makes me sad.

## THE TALK – Q & A

Sickle cell anemia is a blood disorder typically inherited from a person's parent(s). It is more common in people of African origin. Even today, it's not widely discussed as diabetes and cancer; however, this disease also has a high mortality rate.

When my sister Darlene was pregnant with her child, she went into crisis and that's when the doctors informed my parents that she had sickle cell anemia. After her diagnosis, this disease became one of the topics of discussion at our dinner table. A year later, I began throwing up more and being picked up early from school a lot. After one of my extreme vomiting episodes, the school informed my parents that I could not return without a doctor's note. My parents took me to the doctor and I was also diagnosed with this disease at age eleven.

From that moment on, I tried to ask my parents questions because I wanted to know everything there was to know about this disease; however, it was to no avail because not only were they never tested for it, they didn't know much about it. As I got older, I decided to take all my questions to my doctor. The doctor informed me that it would be best to have children with someone who didn't have the disease or the trait; because if I did, there would be a 1 and 4 chance that our children could be susceptible to having this disease.

At that moment, I decided that if I ever have children I needed to know if it would affect them someday. I made the decision that I would stress that they always be aware of their medical history and know how to take care of themselves.

As I watched my children grow, I knew that the day would come for us to have "the talk." I informed them about my health early on because I shared with them that I was very sick during all three pregnancies. They grew up witnessing me being sick. I taught them what to do in case of an emergency. My children knew how to call 911 if I was not able to. Because they were young and saw all the pain I was in, it frightened them.

As they began developing and encountering other people, places, and things, I felt more impressed that "the talk" wouldn't be like the normal good ol' birds and bees one. No, it was going to be in much more detail, on another level, a lot more serious in nature.

I explained to them that I have sickle cell disease and that I inherited it from my parents. Just like the doctors told me, I told them that they have to be very selective, careful, and knowledgeable about whom they choose to have children with. My children took that news well.

Being in the hospital so much, it became second nature for us. My children used to say to each other, "Mommy's sick. We have to go to the hospital." I don't think they fully understood the seriousness of my health issue until my sister (their aunt) died. That is when reality hit them and they realized that having sickle cell was nothing to play with.

Even now that they are older, they still don't like when I'm sick or in the hospital, but they understand it better now. As they are in the beginning stages of relationships and dating, it is my hope and prayer that they keep our conversation about their health in the back of their minds.

I've also told my children that nothing in life is easy and they have to work for everything. I told them to keep their eyes and ears open at all times. Just like my daddy told me, I told them to, "Go down there, mind their business, keep their mouths closed, and come back home." "There" refers to anywhere they go when they leave the house, whether it is to a store, school, library, a friend's house, etc.

Living with sickle cell anemia has not and will never be a walk in the park. It is a daily reminder of choosing how you want your life to be. I decided a long time ago that I was not going to let sickle cell destroy me, so I try to keep a positive mindset.

## WHAT NOW?

As I got older, I began to feel more of the effects of sickle cell anemia. I began to get sick a lot more often. My body began to weaken more. Simple tasks became even more challenging.

I began to experience what I felt was a triple whammy with each crisis. It was no longer me just being in the hospital because of a sickle cell crisis. Now, it was me being in the hospital because I was having a sickle cell crisis, pulmonary hypertension, or AFib, an acute chest syndrome.

With the severity of these added health ailments, mixed with my ongoing health issues, things became so bad that I was no longer able to work and I had to be classified as being disabled. Can you imagine that? Disabled at the age of forty. I've tried to wrap my head around that, but it didn't just sink in automatically. At that point, I became mad at sickle cell. Since I was eleven years old, I felt like every decision in my life had to be considered because of sickle cell. Now, it took my ability to work away.

## GOD'S UNCHANGING HAND

But through it all, I am still holding on to God's unchanging hand. My life's verse is Proverbs 3:5-6: "I will trust in the Lord with all my heart and lean not to my own understanding. In all my ways, I will acknowledge Him and He shall direct my paths." I believe in personalizing the scriptures and making them applicable to my life.

I won't deny that I still tried for years to reason and understand why. *What is this? What is the purpose for all of this?* Then one day, after much reasoning, I reminded myself that there was nothing new under the sun. That notion led me to look in my Bible to see if I could find anything or anyone that could relate to my situation. Matthew 9:20-22 came to mind. It talked about a woman with an issue of blood. For years, I just saw it as a woman having trouble with her menstrual cycle. Then one Sunday morning, while I was driving, that woman's situation dropped in my spirit. At first, I brushed it off, not really making any correlations to why she was on my mind. Like a ton of bricks, it hit me that we had something in common. We both dealt with an "Issue of Blood." My issue of blood, unfortunately, was called sickle cell. And we both have been under the care of many doctors. That revelation wasn't the only thing that was dropped in my spirit. She was healed by touching the hem of Jesus's garment (Matthew 9:20). And I am healed by His stripes, according to Isaiah 53:5. It opened my eyes of understanding and I felt a resurgence of energy.

From that moment forward, I chose to look to the scriptures to provide me with the strength I needed to get through each day. I decided to live in the knowledge that whenever I have a crisis or a day that I am not able to get out of bed due to being in so much pain, I would remember the great Psalmist David. I made a commitment to bless the Lord at all times and praise him continually, despite my situation (Psalm 34:1). I also decided to do exactly what Paul said to do in Ephesians 6:10. He told us to be strong in the Lord and in the power of his might.

Now that I made it to my 50s, I look back over my life and remember the times when I couldn't play outside for long periods of time with my friends because I was too tired. I loved to jump rope, play tag, and hide-and-go-seek. But my absolute favorite game was "Mother, May I?" Those simple childhood games, in my opinion, really taught us a lot about bonding, having manners, and following directions.

## MORE COMPLICATIONS

Living with sickle cell has always made me feel like a freak. I always had to be careful since I never knew when I would be sick.

I think sometimes we take life for granted, not realizing that we must be thankful for every time we move our feet or blink our eyes. We can do nothing on our own. It is by the power of the almighty King Jesus Christ. At the age of fifty-one, I take several pills, every morning and every night, so that I can function daily.

In addition to pain, other things began to develop in my body that brought concern and caused me to go on my knees in prayer even more. Around age forty-eight, my family began to notice that something wasn't quite right with my hearing. At first, I ignored them. Then I said to myself, *I am going to prove them wrong.* I decided to go and have a hearing test done. After the test, I was so surprised to find out that my family was right.

After those results, because I was still in denial, I put off seeing an ear, nose, and throat (ENT) doctor for six months. During that time, I cried, prayed, and cried and prayed some more. So many emotions and thoughts came over me. I was hurt, confused, scared, and couldn't quite put into words what I was feeling. *Wow, sickle cell strikes again. This time it's taken some of my hearing.*

Finally, after much thought and consideration, I went to see the ENT. I was officially diagnosed with having hearing loss. The doctor told me that normally we start hearing at level 0. However, I didn't start hearing until level 40. When I heard those words, I began to weep. All I could think about was how I was going to tell my family about this diagnosis and how high the volume has to be in order for me to hear. And now a new journey began.

My next step was getting hearing aids. I had no idea how expensive they were. After researching, I bought a pair (with no help from my insurance company; that's an out-of-pocket expense). Then, I had to get used to wearing them in and on my ears. But that wasn't the worst part. Learning how to adjust my glasses to this newfound piece of "jewelry" I had to wear was actually the worst part.

I must say this has been a very hard adjustment, not just for me, but also for my family. Losing some of my hearing has really changed the way I look at things that we use our ears for. I have to admit that seeing the closed caption on the television at the doctor's office used to get on my nerves before all this occurred. I don't know why it did. But now, I welcome that very mechanism. I used to use texting when I didn't feel like talking. Now, it has become a necessity. I request people to text me because it is such a struggle to try and hear what is being said while we're on the phone. This can happen because of the feedback whistling noise that I sometimes get from the hearing aids.

After wearing the hearing aids for three years, I knew something still wasn't quite right. I could hear, but I had difficulty making out what people were saying. I still wanted to know more about my hearing loss.

I continued to research and discovered that I never saw an audiologist and didn't know I needed to see one. I called the insurance company to ask for a list of audiologists that were a part of their network.

There was only one audiologist on the list, so I called and made an appointment (which was scheduled for two weeks later). After taking a hearing test at the audiologist's (who was extremely nice, helpful, and had a great bedside manner), I was informed that I have moderate to severe hearing loss. That's when the light bulb came on. *Wow, so my hearing is getting worse?* The hearing aids that I'm currently using are inefficient and I need a better pair. Unfortunately, my insurance company still doesn't cover hearing aids.

The audiologist asked me if I was aware that sickle cell could be the reason for my hearing loss. I told him that I knew because wherever blood flows in your cells you can get sick, which can affect every area of your body some way or another. He smiled and nodded in agreement.

This new diagnosis will not stop my praise. God will still get all the glory. Regardless of the joy and pain that I have experienced living with sickle cell anemia, I will continue to live with a smile on my face, joy in my heart, and a praise on my lips.

# NAVIGATING THROUGH THE JOURNEY

These are some tips that I have learned along the way that have helped me in the medical settings. I believe these can help you as well:

1. Don't be afraid to ask for help.
2. Get to know your primary care doctor so you can feel free to talk to him or her about how you are feeling.
3. Ask about a social worker. They can be very helpful.
4. Know your body.
5. Listen to your body.
6. Ask questions if you don't understand something.
7. Know your blood type.
8. Know your blood count.
9. Know your medications and when to take them.
10. Know the hospital's procedures on treating patients who are having a sickle cell crisis (especially in the emergency room).

# GOD'S SOLUTIONS

The scriptures below are the exact ones I use to help me. I like to read them in the order that I have them listed, because they seem to flow like a letter straight from God to my heart. I hope they give you the same encouragement, hope, and motivation to move forward in any situation.

**Strength and Endurance**
*Proverbs 3:5-6*
*Jeremiah 29:11*
*Deuteronomy 31:6*
*Psalm 103:2-3*

**Encouragement**
*Matthew 5:14-16*
*Luke 11:33-36*
*Acts 22:14-15*
*Philippians 1:9-11*

**In Times of Trouble**
*James 1:2-8*
*1 Thessalonians 5:17-18*
*Psalm 61:1-3*

**Ordered Steps**
*Proverbs 20:24*
*Proverbs 16:2-3*
*Proverbs 16:7-9*

# LETTERS TO MY CHILDREN

*Dear Jocelynn,*

*When I found out that I was pregnant with you a lot of things ran through my mind. I asked myself, Is this really happening, and what am I going to do? Most people worry about money to support the baby. Not me. My worry was if I could make it through to have you.*

*I was very scared because I was not sure how sickle cell was going to show up. I just knew that it would. That is what my struggle was back then. I never worried about money because I knew that God would take care of that.*

*20 plus years later, you still make me proud. You are a well-educated, black woman, and you continue to show me your growth daily. Keep balanced, daughter, with your loving heart and kind spirit. Having you for a daughter is wonderful.*

*My prayer for you is that you be strong, courageous, and do not be afraid. The Lord, our God, will go ahead of you. He will neither fail you, nor forsake you (Deuteronomy 31:6).*

*Jocelynn, my favorite song is "Amazing Grace." I hope that you will share with the world the amazing gift of singing that you have. Please know that when you do, lives will be changed, and God will be pleased.*

*Love,*
*Mom*

*Dear Titus,*

*Wow, where do I begin? Our story started with a lot of uncertainty because man said one thing and God said another. I chose to believe the voice of the Lord, and here we are 19 years later. Son, through the experience of having you, I will say that if you are ever at a crossroad in life and don't know what to do or which direction to go, ALWAYS go to God for your answer.*

*Titus, life has a way of making you think harder, live smarter, and move further than you could ever imagine. There are many lessons you have to learn that I cannot teach you. When those lessons show up, always remember that you are strong and capable enough to handle them.*

*"For I know the thoughts that I think toward you, saith the LORD, thoughts of peace, and not of evil, to give you an expected end" (Jeremiah 29:11).*

*God has a plan for your life and that is why Satan has tried to take you out before you could make your grand entrance into the world. Never forget that I said your name means "to set in order."*

*Having you for a son is a delight. Your personality reminds me of your Uncle Rum – full of fun, lots of laughs, and the life of the party.*

*Just like we did with you, you continued the family tradition by naming your son with your and your father's middle name and initials. Take good care of my grandson, Taylen Alexander, because he is a gift from God to you.*

*Love,*
*Mom*

*Dear Benjamin,*

*Son of my right hand, I remember when it was time for you to enter the world. For some reason, you decided not to come when everyone expected you to. After several different unsuccessful methods by the doctor to help my stalled labor, I decided to do what I knew how to do, which was to pray. After talking to God and to you in my belly for two days, I told the doctor and the nurse that you will be coming on the 4th of July; and that is just what you did.*

*You began your life defying odds and you continue to do so. God has given you a special gift. He wants you to praise and worship him. When he sees you worshipping, you put a smile on his face.*

*My son, continue to make God smile, no matter what is going on in or around you. Continue to Praise and Worship the Lord.*

*"For God so loved the world, that he gave his only begotten Son, that whosoever believeth in him should not perish, but have everlasting life" (John 3:16).*

*Benjamin, you have a call on your life and a special anointing that goes along with it. Continue to walk with Jesus. The road will not be easy; however, you will not be alone, because the Lord will be with you. Trust me, I know, son; He is with me as well.*

*Love,*
*Mom*

# CLOSING PRAYER

*Dear Heavenly Father,*

*Father God, in the name of Jesus, I come before you to say thank you, for you have been good to my family and me down through the years.*

*Father God, if I had 10,000 tongues, I couldn't thank you enough, for your mercy endureth forever.*

*Father God, I ask that you will keep every sickle cell warrior encouraged during trying times, and when they are in a crisis— hospitalized or not— if they began to lose hope, please send someone to remind them that they are not alone and that you love them.*

*Father God, please give them grace to endure to the end of their journey. Don't let them give up on their dreams. Lord, for we know that you alone have all power and you are faithful.*

*Father God, I pray even now that if anyone reading this book doesn't know Jesus as their personal Savior, I invite them to, "Confess with their mouth that Jesus is Lord, believe in their heart that God raised him from the dead, and they will be saved" (Romans 10:9).*

*Father God, teach them to ignore what they see and believe what you've said in your Word.*

*In Jesus' name I pray,*
*Amen.*

# ABOUT THE AUTHOR

Samantha R. Williams was born in West Philadelphia, PA. She was educated in the public school system and graduated from University City High School. She continued her education, receiving an Associate's degree in Paralegal Studies.

Samantha is a born-again Christian. She has studied 15 doctrines and completed several accredited biblical leadership courses. She served as coordinator of a women's ministry for two years. Samantha also served in a public relations ministry for over 10 years.

Samantha wears many hats as a sister, friend, wife, aunt, and daughter. She was the last one of 13 children born to her parents. She is most proud of being the wife of Theodore A. Williams for over 20 years and mother of three children (Jocelynn, Titus, and Benjamin). She is also the beaming grandmother of Taylen A. Williams.

Samantha obeyed the Holy Spirit and homeschooled her sons from second through eighth grade. She believes this helped them to gain academic footing and establish Christian values before releasing them into the public school setting.

Samantha's life verse is Proverbs 3:5-6 which states: "Trust in the Lord with all thine heart; and lean not unto thine own understanding. In all thy ways acknowledge him, and he shall direct thy paths."

Within all that is in her, she still gives God all the glory. No one would guess with all of her spunkiness and positive attitude that she lives with sickle cell anemia.

# RESOURCES

Sickle Cell Anemia

https://www.sicklecelldisease.org

Atrial Fibrillation (AFib)

https://www.heart.org/en/health-topics/atrial-fibrillation/what-is-atrial-fibrillation-afib-or-af

Pulmonary Hypertension

Phassociation.org

www.ingramcontent.com/pod-product-compliance
Lightning Source LLC
Chambersburg PA
CBHW011140290426
44108CB00020B/2700